HIP-HOP & R&B

Culture, Music & Storytelling

Gucci Mane

HIP-HOP & R&B

Culture, Music & Storytelling

Alicia Keys	Jay-Z
Gucci Mane	John Legend
Meek Mill	Lil Wayne
Migos	Nicki Minaj
	Pharrell
Beyoncé	Pitbull
Bruno Mars	Post Malone
Cardi B	Rihanna
Chance the Rapper	The Weeknd
DJ Khaled	Travis Scott
Drake	

MC

MASON CREST

HIP-HOP & R&B
Gucci Mane

Culture, Music & Storytelling

MASON CREST
PO Box 221876, Hollywood, FL 33022
(866) MCP-BOOK (toll-free) • www.masoncrest.com

Copyright © 2022 by Mason Crest, an imprint of National Highlights, Inc. All rights reserved. No part of this publication may be reproduced or transmitted in any form or by any means, electronic or mechanical, including photocopying, recording, taping, or any information storage and retrieval system, without permission in writing from the publisher.

Printed in the United States of America

First printing
9 8 7 6 5 4 3 2 1

ISBN (hardback) 978-1-4222-4627-6
ISBN (series) 978-1-4222-4625-2
ISBN (ebook) 978-1-4222-7187-2

Cataloging-in-Publication Data on file with the Library of Congress

Developed and produced by National Highlights Inc.
Editor: Regency House Publishing Ltd.
Cover Design: Annalisa Gumbrecht, Studio Gumbrecht

QR CODES AND LINKS TO THIRD-PARTY CONTENT

You may gain access to certain third-party content ("Third-Party Sites") by scanning and using the QR Codes that appear in this publication (the "QR Codes"). We do not operate or control in any respect any information, products, or services on such Third-Party Sites linked to by us via the QR Codes included in this publication, and we assume no responsibility for any materials you may access using the QR Codes. Your use of the QR Codes may be subject to terms, limitations, or restrictions set forth in the applicable terms of use or otherwise established by the owners of the Third-Party Sites. Our linking to such Third-Party Sites via the QR Codes does not imply an endorsement or sponsorship of such Third-Party Sites or the information, products, or services offered on or through the Third-Party Sites, nor does it imply an endorsement or sponsorship of this publication by the owners of such Third-Party Sites.

CONTENTS

Chapter 1: Career Highlights—Setting Recording Industry Records 7

Chapter 2: The Road to the Top—Fulfilling a Lifelong Dream 31

Chapter 3: Gucci Mane's Hip-Hop Career, Interests, and Passions in Moments 41

Chapter 4: Gucci Mane's Words, Lyrics, Messaging, and Brand Building..................... 55

Chapter 5: Gucci Mane Reminds Us to Give of Ourselves... 63

Series Glossary of Key Terms 70

Further Reading and Internet Resources 72

Citations 73

Educational Video Links 75

Index 76

Picture and Video Credits 79

Author's Biography 80

KEY ICONS TO LOOK FOR:

Words to Understand: These words with their easy-to-understand definitions will increase the reader's understanding of the text while building vocabulary skills.

Sidebars: This boxed material within the main text allows readers to build knowledge, gain insights, explore possibilities, and broaden their perspectives by weaving together additional information to provide realistic and holistic perspectives.

Educational Videos: Readers can view videos by scanning our QR codes, providing them with additional educational content to supplement the text. Examples include news coverage, moments in history, speeches, iconic sports moments, and much more!

Text-Dependent Questions: These questions send the reader back to the text for more careful attention to the evidence presented there.

Research Projects: Readers are pointed toward areas of further inquiry connected to each chapter. Suggestions are provided for projects that encourage deeper research and analysis.

Series Glossary of Key Terms: This back-of-the-book glossary contains terminology used throughout this series. Words found here increase the reader's ability to read and comprehend higher-level books and articles in this field.

Gucci Mane

HIP-HOP & R&B

Chapter 1

Career Highlights—
Setting Recording Industry Records

Nobody starts their career as a trap pioneer, not even Gucci Mane. At one point, he was a little kid moving to a big city with his mama and older brother.

When his family relocated from Alabama to Georgia during Davis's fourth-grade year, it put him in the right place for his career, but the wrong place for staying out of trouble. By his eighth-grade year, he was rapping, writing poetry, and selling marijuana, something his brother introduced him to as a pocket-change moneymaker. During high school, his deal-making grew to include crack cocaine so he could afford Jordans and a Starter jacket, items the other school kids wore.

He also hit the recording studio before even entering high school, initially attracted to the rap genre by the fashion sense and glamour of Big Daddy Kane and his associates. As an independent artist, he recorded and released the single "Black Tee," which became a local hit. That single peaked the interest of Big Cat Records, which signed him in 2005.

Many in the music industry say that Davis as Gucci Mane would be a "full-on mogul" now,

Big Daddy Kane was an important influence of Davis's early career.

Scan to listen to "Work in Progress," one of the post-reform songs by Gucci Mane.

on the level of Kanye West and Jay-Z, if it had not been for his continued run-ins with the law. He helped launch the rap sub-genre of trap music and, despite his prior problems with drugs and the law, has created one of the most prolific music catalogs of the twenty-first century. Gucci Mane has recorded seventy-two mixtapes alone. Kicked off by his debut album, *Trap House,* on Big Cat Records, he has since recorded fifteen other albums, two collaborative albums, three compilation albums, and one soundtrack. Even during incarcerations, he found a way to produce mixtapes, releasing more than two dozen. That kept fans hungry for a new studio release while he was out of the loop.

His determination earned him respect and status as a genre icon. During his last incarceration, he decided to move his life and career in a more positive direction. His post-release highlights include 2016's *Everybody Looking*, 2017's *Mr. Davis*, and 2019's *Woptober II*. Each charted in the Top 10 of the U.S. Billboard 200.

Diss and Dat

At age twenty-five, his debut album, *Trap House*, charted number one on Billboard's Heatseekers chart. His single "Icy" hit the radio waves and the charts. His beef with fellow hit maker and song collaborator Young Jeezy spawned numerous diss tracks, which helped promote the album in a manner similar to that used by Meek Mill. In the case of Gucci Mane and Young Jeezy, the problem stemmed from an argument over song rights. The copyright conflict held no candle to the mess he found himself in in the Georgia courts though.

Davis's career did not launch in the way he thought it would, though, because in the same month of the album's release, May, he found himself arrested and charged with the murder of a Young Jeezy associate. The dead man was one of a group of five men who illegally entered his friend's home while he was there, threatening to kill Davis. The rapper shot into the group, killing one man. In court, his lawyers argued that he had acted in self-defense. In January of 2006, lacking evidence, the state's prosecutors dropped the charges. He remained in jail until later that month though, held on separate charges that were unrelated to the murder.

Upon his release, Davis immediately returned to the studio and recorded his second album, the aptly named *Hard to Kill,* which he released in October. Re-recording the song "Go Head" from his debut album, he connected the second release to *Trap House* and sought to make up for some of the lost promotion time. He quickly followed up *HTK* with *The State vs. Radric Davis* in December of 2009.

In 2010, the rapper released *The Appeal: Georgia's Most Wanted,* which was chock full of

Scan here to watch "I Get the Bag, featuring Migos," another of Mane's songs from *Mr. Davis.*

Nicki Minaj collaborated with Davis on his album The Appeal: Georgia's Most Wanted.

collaborations with Estelle, Nicki Minaj, and Wyclef. The following year, he issued his "street album," *The Return of Mr. Zone 6* which featured the single "Mouth Full of Gold," a collaboration with Birdman.

In 2011, Gucci Mane decided collaborations were his thing and he released the first of two collaborative albums *1017 Bricksquad Presents ... Ferrari Boyz* which he wrote and recorded with Baytl and Waka Flocka Flame with V-Nasty. The other was a follow up to his mixtape *The State vs. Radric Davis*. Released in 2013, *The State vs. Radric Davis II: The Caged Bird Sings*, offered collaborations with Migos, Peewee Longway, Rocko, Verse Simmonds, Young Dolph, Young Scooter, and Young Thug. The same year also included a falling-out with Waka Flaka Flame, a very public riff that included numerous public tweets.

In late 2013, Davis landed in jail again, that time for a firearms possession charge. He took a plea that resulted in him serving two years in prison. Though he was not paroled until May of 2016, he released nearly thirty mixtapes while incarcerated.

Upon his release, he again headed straight to the studio, releasing his ninth studio album, *Everybody Looking*, in 2016. He issued the album on his newly minted record label, Guwop Enterprises. The collaboration-infused album included recordings with Drake, Kanye West, and Young Thug. His massive mixtape-creation

Davis has also collaborated with Wyclef Jean.

Scan here to listen to Gucci Mane's "Mall."

phase had whetted listeners' appetites, and the album debuted in the number-two slot on the Billboard 200.

He continued creating at a frenetic pace, following up that studio release with a tenth studio album, *Woptober,* a mere five months later. After recording it with super producer Rick Ross, Travis Scott, and Young Dolph, Gucci Mane scored his first Billboard number one with his version of the Rae Sremmurd hit "Black Beatles." Toward the end of 2016, he released a third album, *Return of the East Atlanta Santa*. That release debuted in the Billboard Top 20.

With no plans to slow down, the artist recorded and released the Shawty Redd collaborative extended play *3 for Free* in 2017. His next project, a collaboration with producer Metro Boomin, *Drop Top Wop*, he released on the one-year anniversary of his prison release. It featured collaborations with 2 Chainz, Offset, Rick Ross, and Young Dolph.

He followed the collaborations with another studio album, *Mr. Davis*, which debuted in the second slot on the Billboard 200. It offered fans a plethora of guests, including Migos on "I Get the Bag," Monica on "We Ride," Nicki Minaj on "Make Love," and the Weeknd on "Curve." With music seemingly welling up inside him, Davis continued his creative run, releasing a third album in 2017, *El Gato: The Human Glacier,* produced by the

Southside. It debuted on the Billboard rap chart Top Ten (his eighteenth album to do so) and charted on the Top 30 album chart.

The year 2018 found Davis returning the guest-spot favor. He appeared on Migos' single "CC" and "I Know" with OSBS. He also released his thirteenth studio album, *Evil Genius*, a star-studded affair that brought together 21 Savage, Bruno Mars, Kevin Gates, Lil Yachty, Migos, and Quavo. He followed it up with *Delusions of Grandeur*, which charted in the Top Ten of the Billboard 200, his fifth album to do so. Another star-studded affair to accompany the previous year's, he brought together Anuel AA, Justin Bieber, and Meek Mill. Not yet done creatively for the year, he released a mixtape sequel—*Woptober II*. On it, he collaborated with artists he had not previously

Scan here to listen to Gucci Mane's "Cold Shoulder."

Davis is a hard worker, having produced a large number of albums.

worked with—DaBaby, Lil Baby, Megan Thee Stallion, and YoungBoy Never Broke Again. The mixtape included two singles, "Big Booty" and "Richer Than Errybody." Toward the end of 2019, Davis issued another holiday mixtape, *East Atlanta Santa 3*.

All Released Solo Albums to Date:
Discography

LA FLARE
(Released June 5, 2001)

Davis released an independent "street album," *La Flare*, as a demo to land gigs. It had an extremely small pressing of 1,000 copies on compact disc (CD). The self-financed debut helped him land his first local club dates.

TRAP HOUSE
(Released May 24, 2005)

His first major label release charted at number 10 on Billboard's U.S. Rap chart. His hit single "Icy," performed with Young Jeezy, helped him land his first national listeners.

Collaborations
- "Icy" featuring Young Jeezy and Boo
- "Go Head" featuring Mac Bre-Z

Scan the code to watch Gucci Mane's mixtape single release "Aggressive."

HARD TO KILL
(Released October 10, 2006)

Recorded during the period of February to early fall of 2006, his follow-up to his first major label debut featured raps that centered around his survived assassination attempt and his first incarceration.

Collaborations
- "My Chain," featuring Black Magic
- "Pillz," featuring Mac Bre-Z
- "Go Head," featuring Mac Bre-Z
- "Drive Fast," featuring Jason Caesar
- "Stick Em Up," featuring La Chat
- "We Live This," featuring Black Magic and Young Snead
- "Trap Gurl," featuring Gangsta Boo

TRAP-A-THON
(Released September 4, 2007)

His third album release became his first that was chock full of collaborations. The artist quickly made contacts within rap and fostered positive working relationships across genres.

Collaborations
- "Bling Bling," featuring Big Tank
- "Re-Up," featuring Yatta Mann
- "What They Do," featuring Young Snead & Khia

Bruno Mars worked with Davis on his album *Evil Genius*.

- "Aw-Man," featuring .45
- "Choppa Shoppin'," featuring Maceo, Young Snead & Black Magic
- "Bad Guys," featuring Black Magic
- "Pillz (Remix)," featuring Big Tank

Back to the Trap House
(Released October 2, 2007)

His fourth release continued this collaborative process of creation. On it, he introduced new collaborators and expanded his creative Rolodex.

Collaborations
- "Freaky Gurl" (Remix), featuring Lil Kim and Ludacris
- "I Know Why," featuring Pimp C, Rich Boy and Blaze-1
- "I Might Be," featuring Shawnna and Game
- "Drink It Straight," featuring Trey Songz
- "Jump the Line," featuring Young Gunna
- "G-Love (You Don't Love Me)," featuring LeToya Luckett
- "Ballers," featuring Shawnna

Murder Was the Case
(Released May 5, 2009)

Gucci Mane earned his third-highest chart album position with *Murder Was the Case*. It debuted at number twenty-three on the Top 200 Billboard album chart.

Scan here to listen to Gucci Mane's "Both" (feat. Drake)

Lil Kim collaborated with Davis on "Freaky Gurl" (remix).

Collaborations
- "Murder for Fun," (Young Jeezy Diss) featuring Ox
- "Trap Money," (Remix) featuring B.A. & Mook
- "Get Low (Like a Lambo)," featuring Selassie
- "Gangs," featuring Biz

THE STATE VS. RADRIC DAVIS
(Released December 8, 2009)

While the album went gold, as certified by RIAA, three of its singles went platinum—"Wasted," "Spotlight," and "Lemonade"

Collaborations
- "Wasted," featuring Plies
- "Spotlight," featuring Usher
- "Bingo," featuring Soulja Boy and Waka Flocka Flame

THE APPEAL: GEORGIA'S MOST WANTED
(Released September 28, 2010)

The sequel to 2009's *The State vs. Radric Davis* debuted at number four on the Billboard Top 200 album chart.

Davis collaborated with Soulja Boy on "Bingo".

Collaborations

- "Little Friend," featuring Bun B
- "Gucci Time," featuring Swizz Beatz
- "Remember When," featuring Ray J
- "Haterade," featuring Pharrell & Nicki Minaj
- "It's Alive," featuring Swizz Beatz
- "ODog," featuring Wyclef
- "Grown Man," featuring Estelle

THE RETURN OF MR. ZONE 6
(Released March 22, 2011)

The critically acclaimed album featured another slew of collaborations. The much-anticipated work debuted on the Billboard Top 200 album chart at number eighteen. On the Billboard Top Rap Albums chart, it entered at number two.

Collaborations

- "Mouth Full of Golds," featuring Birdman
- "This Is What I Do," featuring Waka Flocka Flame and OJ da Juiceman
- "Reckless," featuring Cap and Chill Will
- "Shout Out to My Set," featuring Wooh Da Kid
- "I Don't Love Her," featuring Rocko and Webbie
- "Brinks," featuring Master P
- "Pretty Bitches," featuring Wale

Pharrell Williams collaborated with Davis on his album The Appeal: Georgia's Most Wanted.

Rap artist Waka Flocka Flame features on Davis's track "Trick or Treat" and "Pancakes."

- "Pancakes," featuring Waka Flocka Flame and 8Ball
- "Hell Yeah," featuring Slim Dunkin
- "Trick or Treat," featuring Slim Dunkin, Wooh Da Kid and Waka Flocka Flame

Everybody Looking
(Released July 22, 2016)

One of his post-prison releases, the album features his first collaboration with Canadian artist Drake.

Collaborations
- "Back on Road," featuring Drake
- "Guwop Home," featuring Young Thug

The Return of East Atlanta Santa
(Released December 16, 2016)

This album became the first released on his GUWOP label imprint, a partnership with Atlantic Records. More playful than prior releases, it included a follow-up collaboration with Drake.

Collaborations
- "Both," featuring Drake
- "Drove U Crazy," featuring Bryson Tiller
- "Last Time," featuring Travis Scott

Mr. Davis
(Released October 13, 2017)

This is the most recent album release of the artist to go gold as certified by RIAA. The critically acclaimed album featured near constant collaborations, but they were artfully woven into the creative fabric, so they did not alter Gucci Mane's signature flow.

Scan here to listen to Gucci Mane's "Lemonade."

Collaborations

- "I Get the Bag," featuring Migos
- "Stunting Ain't Nuthin," featuring Slim Jxmmi and Young Dolph
- "Curve," featuring The Weeknd
- "Enormous," featuring Ty Dolla Sign

EL GATO: THE HUMAN GLACIER
(Released December 22, 2017)

El Gato stands out among Davis's many works for a few reasons. The critically acclaimed album was written solely by the trio of Davis, Joshua Luellen (aka Southside), and Jacob Dutton (aka Jake One) and recorded in a mere two days. The comedic tones to the album made it a favorite among critics. The album also stands out because it features no guest appearances or collaborations beyond those of its core songwriters. Luellen produced every track.

EVIL GENIUS
(Released December 7, 2018)

The album *Evil Genius* features Gucci Mane's biggest hit so far as measured by sales. The single "Wake Up in the Sky," with Bruno Mars and Kodak Black, has been certified as triple platinum by the RIAA. That means that the single has sold at least three million units.

Scan here listen to "Wake Up in The Sky" (feat. Bruno Mars and Kodak Black).

Davis collaborated with The Weeknd on "Curve."

Collaborations

- "Solitaire," featuring Migos and Lil Yachty
- "Kept Back," featuring Lil Pump
- "Wake Up in the Sky," with Bruno Mars and Kodak Black

Delusions of Grandeur
(Released June 21, 2019)

The album debuted at number seven on the Billboard Top 200 album chart. It features surprising collaborations, including one with Justin Bieber.

Collaborations

- "Love Thru the Computer," featuring Justin Bieber
- "Backwards," featuring Meek Mill

Woptober II
(Released October 18, 2019)

Davis created a group project that consisted solely of collaborations in which every song was co-written, and guests appeared on more than half the tracks. Every track had a different producer with Gucci Mane as the executive producer. The much anticipated album debuted at number nine on the Billboard Top 200 album chart.

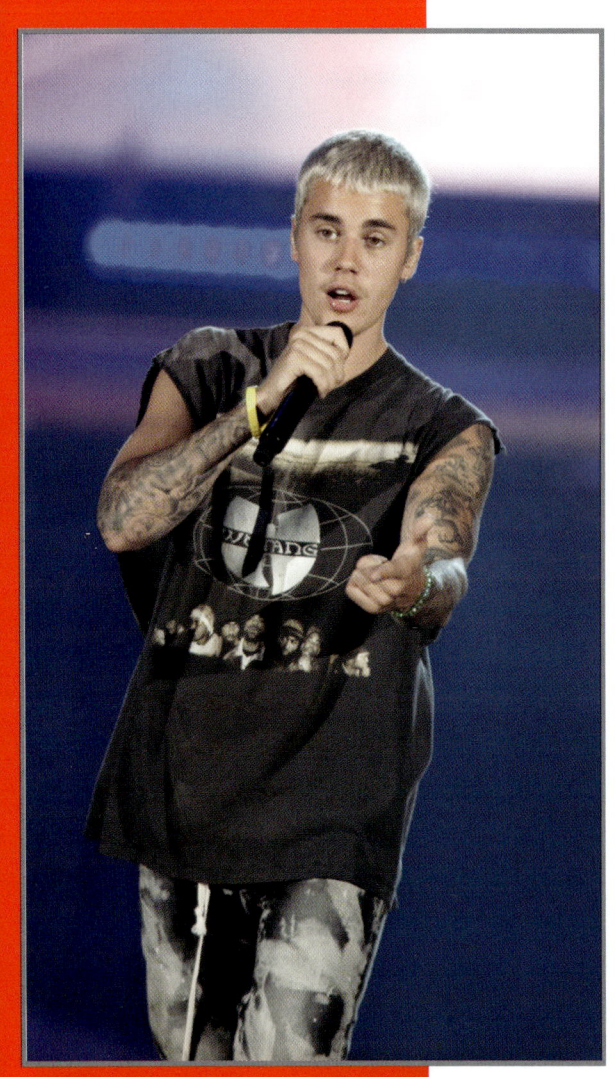

Davis collaborated with Justin Bieber on Delusions of Grandeur.

Collaborations
- "Richer Than Errybody," featuring YoungBoy Never Broke Again and DaBaby
- "Big Booty," featuring Megan Thee Stallion
- "Tootsies," featuring Lil Baby

EAST ATLANTA SANTA 3
(Released December 20, 2019)

With his final release of 2019, the artist brought out the third of his East Atlanta Santa series. By that time, the holiday-themed releases had become fan favorites.

Collaborations
- "Drummer," featuring Kranium
- "More," with Jason Derulo
- "Magic City," featuring Asian Doll
- "She Miss Me," featuring Rich the Kid
- "Tony," featuring Quavo
- "Slide," featuring Quavo

Quavo, who is also a member of Migos, collaborated with Davis on *East Atlanta Santa 3*.

Mixtapes

Gucci Mane not only pioneered trap music, he took mixtapes to a new level. From his first mixtape, *Chicken Talk* in 2006 to his most recent at publication, *Drop Top Wop*, released in 2017, he has written, recorded and produced at a manic level. To date, the artist Gucci Mane has released 72 mixtapes. Here are just some of them.

Chicken Talk, released October 11, 2006
Ice Attack, released February 26, 2007
No Pad, No Pencil, released November 10, 2007
EA Sportscenter, released May 1, 2008
Mr. Perfect, released May 22, 2008
Bird Flu: Part 2, released January 29, 2009
The Cold War: Part 1 (Guccimerica), released October 17, 2009
The Cold War: Part 2 (Great Brrritain), released October 17, 2009
The Cold War: Part 3 (Brrrussia), released October 17, 2009
Burrrprint (2) HD, released March 13, 2010
Mr. Zone 6, released June 19, 2010
Gucci 2 Time, released January 14, 2011
Bricksquad Mafia (with 1017 Brick Squad), released February 5, 2011
Writings on the Wall 2, released July 5, 2011
Trap Back, released February 5, 2012
I'm Up, released May 25, 2012
EastAtlantaMemphis (with Young Dolph), released March 15, 2013
Trap Back 2, released March 15, 2013
World War 3: Molly (with Metro Boomin, Sonny Digital and Dun Deal), released August 13, 2013
World War 3: Gas (with 808 Mafia), released August 13, 2013

Diary of a Trap God, released September 11, 2013
Trust God Fuck 12 (with Rich Homie Quan), released October 19, 2013
Young Thugga Mane La Flare (with Young Thug), released April 20, 2014
Brick Factory Vol. 1, released May 26, 2014
World War 3D: The Green Album (with Migos), released: June 16, 2014
World War 3D: The Purple Album (with Young Thug), released June 16, 2014
Trap House 4, released July 4, 2014
Felix Brothers (with Young Dolph & Peewee Longway as Felix Brothers), released July 17, 2014
The Oddfather, released July 28, 2014
Gucci Vs. Guwop, released August 15, 2014
Brick Factory Vol. 2, released September 3, 2014
The Return of Mr. Perfect, released September 13, 2014
Trap God 3, released October 17, 2014
Big Gucci Sosa (with Chief Keef), released October 30, 2014
East Atlanta Santa, released December 25, 2014
C.N.O.T.E. Vs. Gucci (with Honorable C.N.O.T.E.), released December 25, 2014
1017 Mafia: Incarcerated, released January 3, 2015
Brick Factory 3, released February 12, 2015
Mr. Clean, The Middle Man, released March 4, 2015
Breakfast, released March 17, 2015
Lunch, released March 17, 2015
Dinner, released March 17, 2015
Trap House 5 (The Final Chapter), released April 6, 2015
King Gucci, released May 20, 2015
Mamas Basement (with Zaytoven), released January 27, 2016
C-Note vs. Gucci 2 (with Honorable C-Note), released February 19, 2016
Woptober, released October 14, 2016
Droptopwop, released May 26, 2017

The Inside Skinny on Some Major Collaborations

With each album and performance, Gucci Mane illustrates his love of music. He writes constantly and frequently collaborates with a wide variety of musicians and rappers. His frequent collaborators include Rick Ross, Drake, and 2 Chainz.

Frequent Collaborator and Producer

"Gucci Mane is one of the most street guys I ever met. But when he raps, it sounds like nursery rhymes." — producer Zaytoven

Working Together on DropTopWizop
(Released 2017)

"I've been a huge Gucci fan my whole life. I used to bump the classic Gucci and all that. I feel like with me going out to Miami and connecting with him in his space at the beginning of the year, I feel like that was a big moment in my career. Just being able to lock in with him, make beats, work with him, and knock out stuff for the album was really a good experience. At the same time, you

Davis at the BET Hip Hop Awards in 2016.

feel like you're a big part of the album." Shane Lindstrom (aka Murda Beatz) told *Billboard*.

Tours Completed

As prolifically as he records, Gucci Mane rarely tours. He plays occasional dates, typically large festivals. He has festival concert performances scheduled for 2020 and 2021.

THE *APPEAL* TOUR

Davis played small club dates during 2010 in support of his album *The Appeal: Georgia's Most Wanted*. The album spawned the hit single "Gucci Time" and had the highest debut at the time of any of the rapper's releases, so he hit the road to earn it more sales.

THE *TRAP GOD* TOUR

Kicked off on April 5th, 2017, in Boston, Massachusetts, Davis toured the U.S. in his first-ever road tour. Prior to the tour, he had only played scattered dates at small venues.

THE *LIVE IN CANADA* TOUR

In May of 2019, Gucci Mane toured Canada, playing ten dates. He featured Canadian musicians Merkules and Peter Jackson as his opening acts. The tour began in Halifax on May 15th and ended May 31th in Winnipeg. American musician August Alsina played all but three of the dates as well.

American musician August Alsina played some dates on Davis's *Live in Canada* tour. Here he is at the 2017 BET Awards with Queen Latifah.

Words to Understand

Extricate: To release or free a person, animal, or thing from entanglement or a situation.

Hustle: In business, to aggressively sell a product or service; in U.S. street slang, to swindle or con someone.

Mannerisms: Habitual speech or gestures of an individual.

Shotgun house: A lengthy, narrow, rectangular style of home, native to the Deep South, typically about twelve feet wide with the interior rooms behind one another and exterior doors on either end of the home.

Davis at the 2017 BET Awards.

Chapter 2:

The Road to the Top—
Fulfilling a Lifelong Dream

While the rapper known as Gucci Mane now calls Georgia home, the man born Radric Delantic Davis in Bessemer, Alabama, spent his early childhood in Birmingham, Alabama. Born on February 12th, 1980 to Ralph Everett Dudley and Vicky Dean Davis, he took his mother's surname, as did his brother Victor.

Both his father and his grandfather, James Dudley Sr., had served in the military, but it was his mother's career as a social worker and teacher that precipitated the family's move to Atlanta when Davis was a fourth-grader. That move put him in the right place for his career but the wrong place for staying out of trouble.

Davis was born in Birmingham, AL.

A Major Relocation

Leaving Alabama meant leaving the only school and friends he had known. Davis had attended Jonesboro Elementary for both kindergarten and elementary school, where his teachers had encouraged his poetry writing. He and his family left the small, encouraging city of Birmingham for the metropolitan Atlanta.

Fast Fact 1:

Poetry—Radric Davis's childhood interest in poetry writing has helped poetry become a more popular reading pastime. In the UK, poetry has become more popular with teenagers and Millennials. According to Nielsen BookScan, poetry sales grew by more than 12 percent last year. That was the second year in a row that such growth has occurred. If you would like to try writing poetry, you first need to determine which kind you want to write: narrative, haiku, limerick, free verse, or lyrical poetry.

Life in Atlanta began rough. The Davis family had a tough time finding affordable housing. For a time, they lived in a Knights Inn. The iffy neighborhood first exposed his brother, then him, to the drug trade. The neighborhood also exposed him to rap though, and music became his saving grace.

Young Davis watched the original Gucci Mane, his dad, **hustle** on Atlanta's streets. Radric Davis took his stage name from his father. As a child, he was known as Lil Gucci.

"You know, he had all kinds of games and scams, like three card molly, shaking the pea, pigeon drop," Davis said to NPR in an interview with reporter Ailsa Chang. "All of these are little scams that he learned are tricks of the trade that he learned in the streets."

Davis studied his father's trade and combined the knowledge with what he learned from his brother. His street-wise earnings funded his first forays into music and provided the fodder for the songs. His accurate depictions of the drug trade and trap life, including the home life and women who date those in the drug trade, earned him a reputation as a "rapper who keeps in real," as *Married Biography* put it.

From watching his dad, he learned to stay aware. "He just was kind of like, always on point, or trying to be as sharp as he can or, you

Davis's move to Atlanta with his family did not start well, when he embarked on a life of drugs, but an interest in rap kick-started his music career.

know, read when trouble was coming," he told NPR. "I just watched his nature, and I watched his **mannerisms**. He didn't really teach it to me, but I kind of adapted to it, because I seen it."

Street Realities

The realities of life in Atlanta, in a neighborhood of **shotgun houses** full of people without "good shoes on their feet," made an indelible mark on him. He became, in his own words, "obsessed with money" and determined to always have it, so he could avoid the related struggles. He realized as a teenager how important earning a good living is and that as long as he did so, he would not become a burden to his family. That became an overarching goal for him.

As he describes in his autobiography and related to NPR in an interview after its release, "I went to sleep hungry, and I knew what it was like to be poor; I knew what it was like to have your lights off, or to have to boil water to take a bath. And that never left me. I seen the way everything was about a dollar. I seen how it could just tear up a whole household. So, in my mind it was always like, try to make yourself not be a burden on nobody. Try to keep yourself at least financially independent enough where you're not a burden on your family, because they don't got it."

Scan here to watch the video of Malcolm Gladwell interviewing Gucci Mane about his transformation.

Davis grew up in poverty, which drove him to seek a better life that he achieved through music.

Davis might have seemed wild on paper, but his enterprising salesmanship was all about the money. The rapper proved a studious nerd, who, while he wrote and recorded his early music, also hit the books, graduating from Ronald E. McNair High School in 1998 with a 3.0 GPA. Davis earned a scholarship to Georgia Perimeter College, but before finishing his bachelor's degree he left school to pursue music.

His first taste of rap success showed him a better way than street life and hustling. Davis became determined to earn his living from music.

"[I decided,] this is what I'm going to do. I don't want to sell drugs no more … I want to be a professional rapper."

Prison Saved Him

What seemed normal in his new neighborhood became the trap that trapped one of trap music's founders. Davis found himself ensconced in a world of drugs and violence that continued to suck him back in each time he attempted to **extricate** himself. He continually landed in prison, a

Davis gained a bachelor's degree from Georgia Perimeter College.

cycle he finally broke during his two-year stint from 2014 to 2016, when he says prison saved his life.

During his last incarceration, he cleaned up from drugs, recommitted himself to his career, and decided to marry the woman he first saw during his third incarceration. While watching television in prison in 2009, he saw a video starring Jamaican model Keyshia Ka'Oir.

He first developed a crush, looking at pictures of her, and made it a point to meet her after his release. He hired her for his 2010 music video "911 Emergency." Captivated by Ka'Oir, the two dated briefly before Davis proposed. The couple married on October 17th, 2017, creating a blended family of her three children and Davis's twelve-year-old son, Bam, from his prior relationship with Sheena Evans. "I may have first fell for her beauty, ogling her pictures while I was sitting in the clink, but I quickly began to appreciate her as a person," Davis wrote in his autobiography.

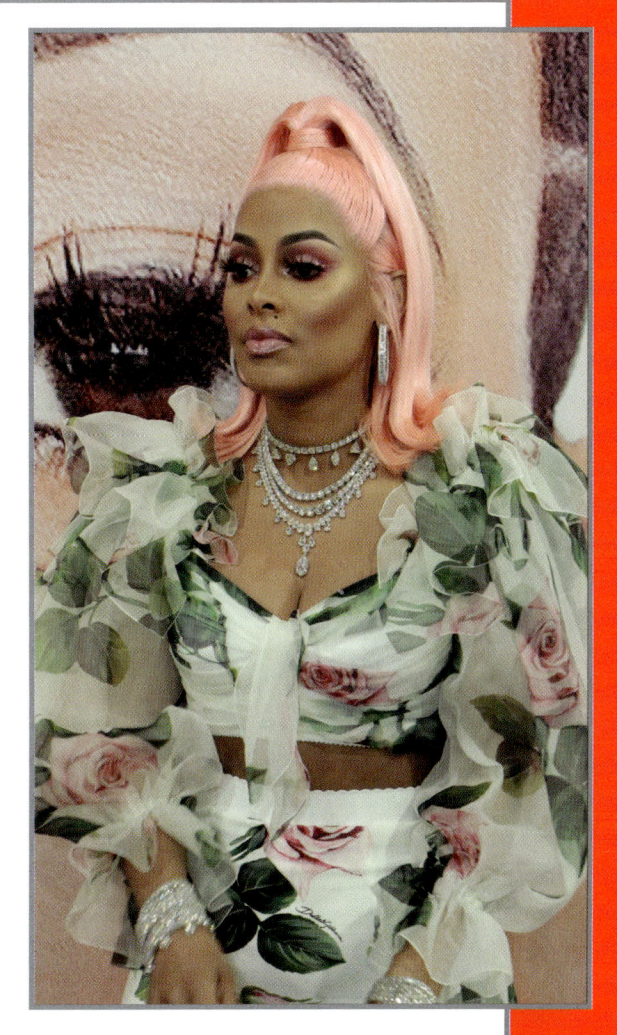

Davis became captivated by Jamaican model Keyshia Ka'Oir.

Becoming Gucci Mane

Shotgun houses, street hustles, and weed sales all combined to provide Radric Davis with the topics for his raps. Davis created a way to express the realities of his and his friends' and families' day-to-day lives by creating the trap music genre. Founding a new music form helped him express his creativity and escape from the mean streets to the nice life.

The hardship of Davis's early life influenced his music and career.

Text-Dependent Questions:

1. At what school did Gucci Mane's teachers encourage his poetry writing?

2. Who taught the rapper to be streetwise and always aware?

3. What college did the artist attend before founding trap music?

Research Project:

Research poetry forms. What are the five most common forms of poetry? Which form bears closest resemblance to that of a rap song form?

Words to Understand

Autobiography: A self-authored story of a person's life.

Career diversification: The practice of maintaining multiple career fields and streams of income.

Haute couture: A French phrase literally translated as "high dressmaking," which in modern meaning refers to one-of-a-kind, high fashion clothing created by designers.

Underdog story: The story of an individual, group, or team that is believed to have little chance to win, but perseveres to triumph.

Davis performing at the 515 Alive Music Festival.

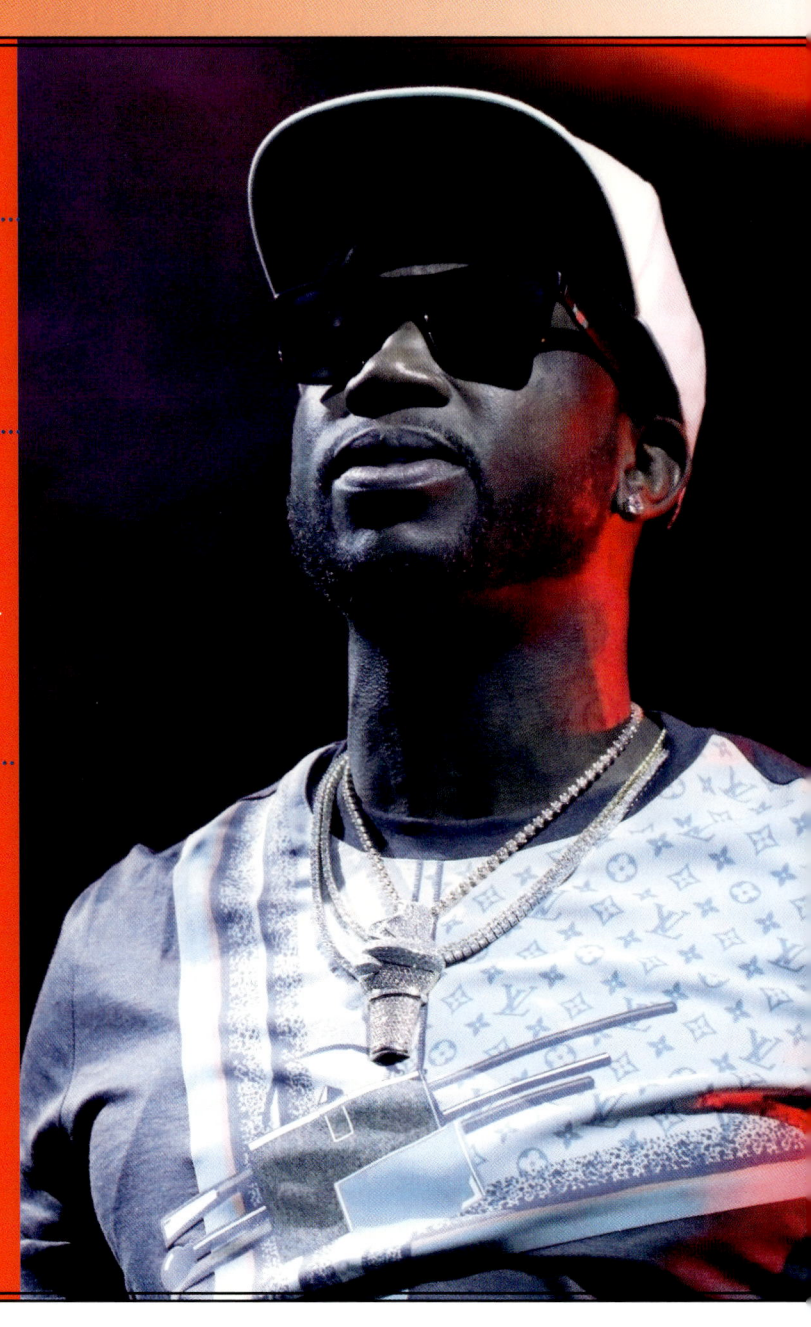

Chapter 3:
Gucci Mane's Hip-Hop Career, Interests, and Passions in Moments

More Than Just a Musician

"If a man does not have the sauce, then he is lost," Davis said. "But the same man can be lost in the sauce."

Essentially, the rapper says, one should have self-confidence and talent but avoid getting a big head. He knows that high-quality productivity comprises a key part of the success of the Gucci Mane brand. He produces high-quality work in the areas of acting, business, music, and writing.

The Actor Life

Davis has amassed a short resume of acting credits, appearing in the movies "Confession of a Thug," "Spring Breaker," "Visual Reality," "Birds of a Feather," and "Beef 4."

His budding acting career stemmed from friendships with directors. Sometimes it has come the long way around. Musician Mariah Carey introduced him to Brett Ratner, who then introduced him to

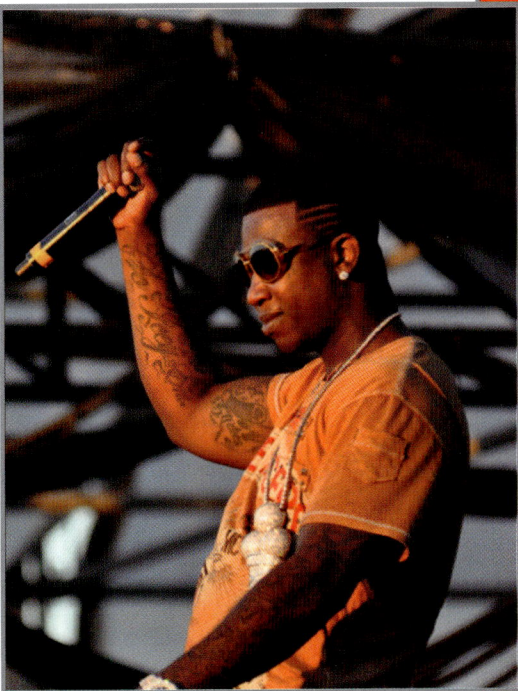

Davis performing at the Williamsburg Waterfront, Brooklyn, New York City.

Davis was introduced to American film director Harmony Korine who gave him a part in his film *Spring Breakers*.

Harmony Korine. That connection has spawned a music video and two film projects for him.

Davis did not start out with an idea to add a career, but he did want to try acting. He thought it needed to be the right part—something streetwise—a "character who made sense and paralleled my life a little bit."

He found that in the bad guy role of Archie in Korine's film *Spring Breakers*. His friend offered up the notion of working together, and he accepted. He paid no mind to his existing schedule, which spawned some amusing moments on film sets. For example, Davis actually fell asleep while filming a romantic scene. His character was supposed to be romancing another character. It was supposed to be a steamy scene … and Davis, exhausted from performing a show earlier that evening in St. Petersburg, fell asleep while shooting.

The remainder of his projects have been less eventful. He did have to learn that he does not get to actually kiss the actresses

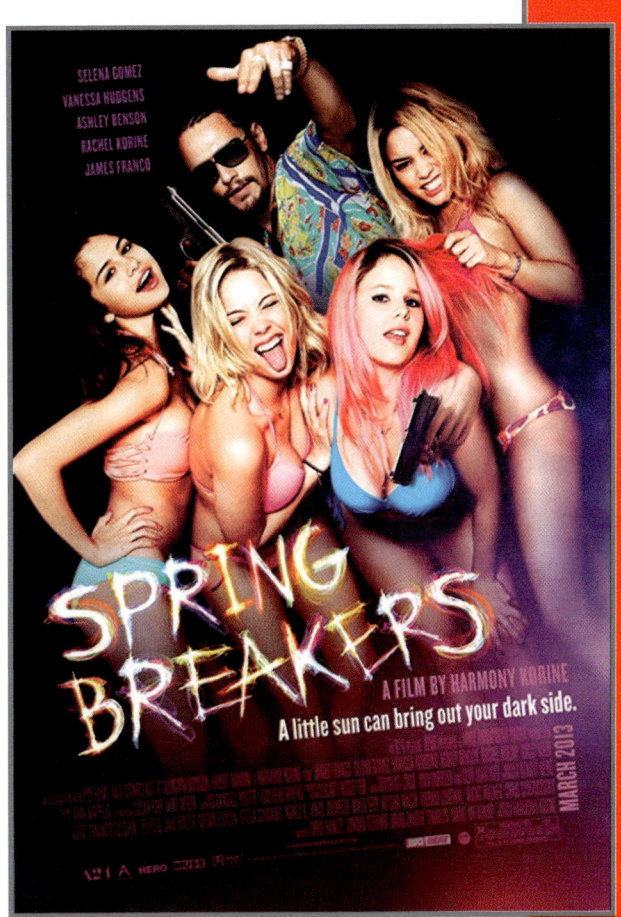

A promotional poster for the film *Spring Breakers* in which Davis played a bad guy.

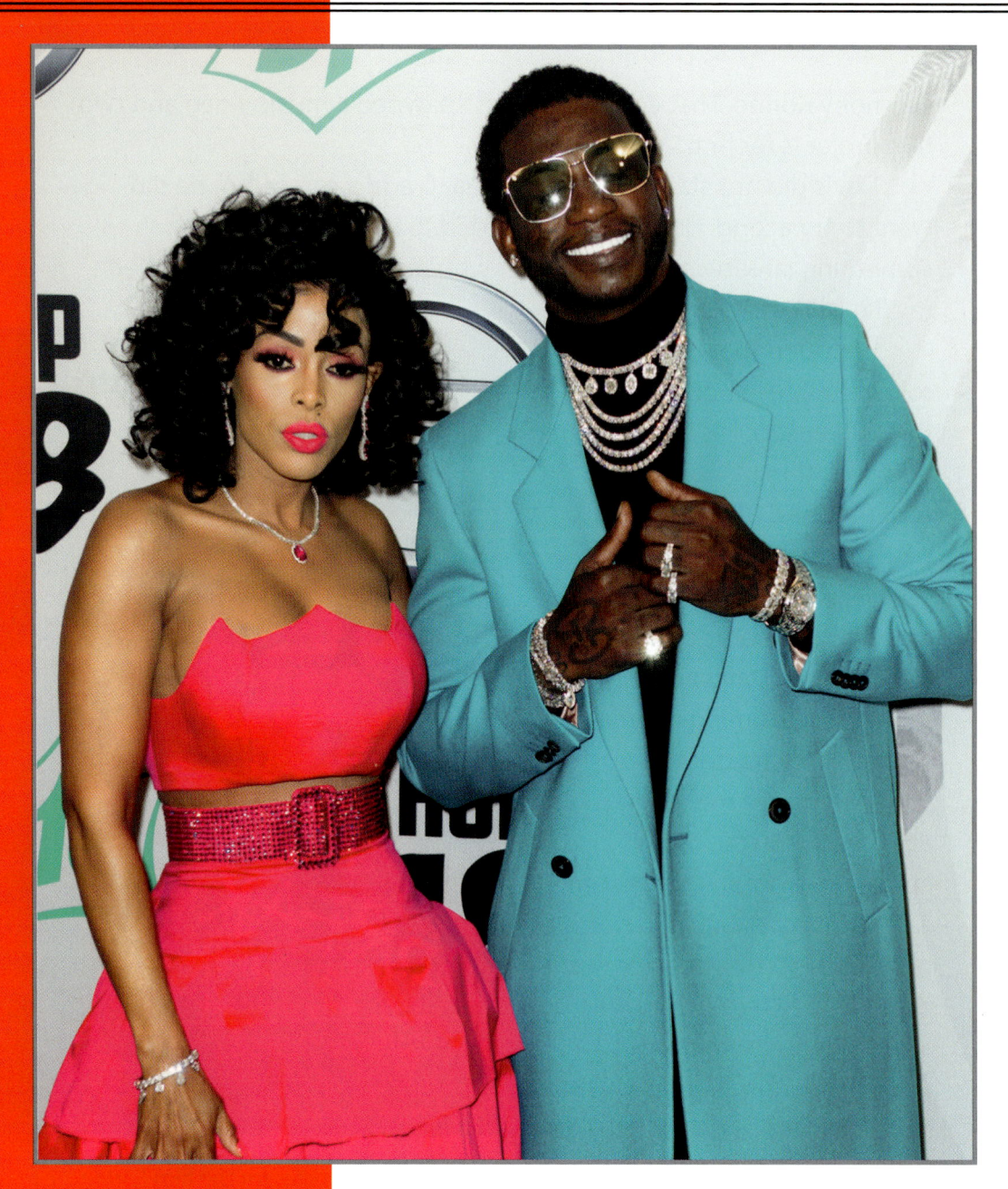

Davis and his wife and model Keyshia Ka'Oir.

44 Gucci Mane HIP-HOP & R&B

Fast Fact 2:

Children's Issues—Many major issues affect individuals under the age of eighteen today. This set of social and economic issues often gets described as "children's issues." This broad term describes a wide array of problems including sexual and physical abuse, cancer, medical needs, homelessness, hunger, education, disabilities, bullying, infant and child mortality, AIDS, mental health problems, teen pregnancy, substance abuse, runaways, educational and employment deficits, neglect, and the foster and adoption systems. Both government agencies, like the U.S. Department of Health and Human Services, and non-profits, like World of Children, work to fund solutions to these problems and to provide direct services.

in love scenes though. He tried, but was told, "Stage kissing only." Everything romantic must be simulated when filming a movie or TV show.

Besides music and acting, Davis also writes. While he focussed on poetry as a child, he now writes non-fiction. Davis authored his **autobiography** during his final incarceration.

The Author Life

The decision to become an author was not brought on by thoughts of **career diversification**. His 2013 arrest did not land him any jail time until 2014, but it did make him think. He had met the woman he would eventually marry, and his career had taken off. The arrest put him into a new mode of thinking.

"I was facing a bunch of time … that, right there, is what made me come to the decision that I need to change my life."

Davis decided, he says, "I'm gonna start doing better."

His time in a federal penitentiary provided him time to read and reflect on life. He chose to read biographies of those who had influenced him. Those included biographies on country musician Johnny Cash, boxer Mike Tyson, and psychedelic musician Jimi Hendrix. It was as he read the second Hendrix biography that he realized his vision to write his own story.

"I just started writing," he said in an interview with NPR, "and I wrote like thirty, forty pages my first time when I sat down to write the book."

He authored an authentic, gritty piece. In the book, he admits his mistakes without glossing over them. He admits to the mistakes he made in his career, too, taking it for granted. He openly discusses the addiction he beat to a drug called "lean," a cough syrup comprising codeine with promethazine. Typically blended with soda pop, Davis says his addiction "derailed my career" for a few years. He beat the addiction while incarcerated though. Upon his release, he has continued to live the sober life.

"I'm having more fun sober, because I can feel everything," he told *GQ* magazine. "When I was high, I was going through the motions. Now everything is fun to me. I can feel the love. I feel excitement."

Scan here to watch the second part of Malcolm Gladwell's interview with Gucci Mane.

The Business Life

Davis also lives the business life. He founded 1017 Records and later partnered with Waka Flocka Flame, who had founded Brick Squad Records, to create the merged label of 1017 Brick Squad Records. Despite their business partnership, the two began a confusing feud, the upshot of which became Waka Flocka Flame's vow that the two would never work together again. Numerous artists call the label home, including OJ Da Juiceman, Waka Flocka Flame, Wooh Da Kid, Young Scooter, and Young Dolph.

Besides the record label imprint he created with the major label that signed him, he founded an athletic wear company, Delantic. The name comes from his middle name. The company has brought out three lines, or "drops," so far.

Davis partnered on the clothing line with 300 Management co-founder Todd Moscowitz, who describes the

Waka Flocka Flame founded Brick Squad Records with Davis.

clothes as "between Supreme and Vetements." Some shirts feature text, some graphics. One sold-out graphic t-shirt features a caricature of Davis as Gucci Mane. Unlike many celebrities who create a clothing line, Davis has kept the cost to consumers reasonable. No shirt costs more than $40.

"We just trying to make a super-duper dope clothing line," Davis told *GQ*. "Exclusive. Super trend. Super hip. Well made. Well crafted. Something that you be proud to spend your money on, and when you get it, you really got a collector's item."

The Family Life

In 2017, he further diversified his life. He added husband and father to the growing list of positions he holds. The man who watched his dad hustle and founded trap music runs a pretty strict household.

Now married, he parents his son and his three step-children from his wife's prior relationships. The family live under one roof. He and model wife Keyshia Ka'Oir agree on the importance of keeping their four children out of the limelight.

Neither parent posts photos of the children to social media. All four kids attend a normal, local school. His son and one of Ka'Oir's children are in elementary school. Keyshia also has a child in junior high school and one in high school. The blended family of two career parents live a normal life, other than the jobs that put Davis and Ka'Oir in the public eye. Davis briefly discusses Bam's birth and their relationship in his book, but he refrains from discussing his step-children or parenting them, out of respect for Ka'Oir and her desire for privacy for herself and her offspring.

"It's a situation where I am proud to be a mother, but, at the same time, I need it to be private," Ka'Oir told *Essence* in an interview. "I don't want them in the limelight. I don't want them to be on social media. I need them to go to school and to just be children."

Davis says he hopes that people read the autobiography, not for a glorification of how he started out, but to read an **underdog story** that could give them hope and inspiration to turn things around, too.

"I been jumping hurdles my whole life," the rapper says. "[It's to] let them know, 'If he can do that, it's never too late for me to turn my life around, because look what he did.'"

Endorsements

You could argue that Gucci Mane's popularity stems from his authenticity as much as from his talent. While many performers have a marketing team and slant, Mane remains a down-to-earth individual.

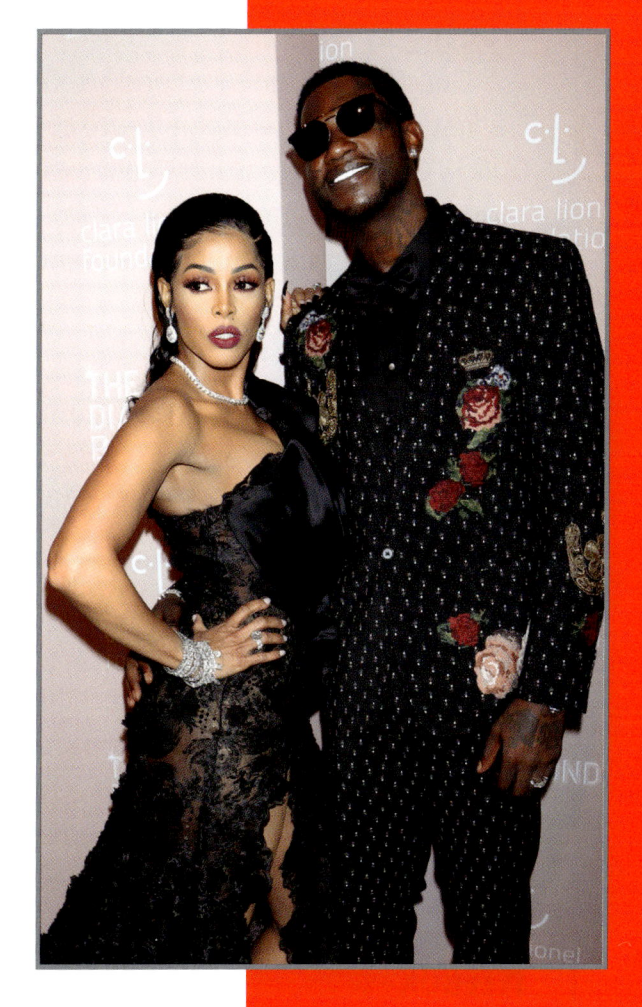

Davis and his wife have a strict policy of keeping their children out of the media, insisting they have normal upbringing.

Gucci

Gucci Mane signed an endorsement contract with Gucci in 2019. His first campaign with the **haute couture** brand comes out in 2020. Gucci's Cruise line features Davis in a "Come as You Are RSVP" campaign. The layout features Gucci Mane in a mansion house party setting with actress Sienna Miller and punk rock singer Iggy Pop.

Supreme

Davis filmed a music video commercial for streetwear brand Supreme. In it, he advocates online shopping and says he does not go to the store—he pushes a button and has his purchases delivered to his home.

Footaction

As much as he loves sneakers, his Footaction campaign had nothing to do with shoes. Davis partnered with Footaction in a campaign to encourage children and youth to develop their business savvy and an entrepreneurial mindset. He joined MadeinTYO and Cousin Stizz in the campaign entitled "Summer Hustle."

Reebok

On the other hand, Davis did ink a deal with Reebok Classic to represent its Workout Plus sneaker. He modeled in ads for the sneakers and designed the **Guwop DMX Run 10**.

Awards Won

While performing as Gucci Mane, Davis has earned many hit singles and placed a number of albums at the top of the rap and overall charts. His extended stints away from music have kept him from winning many awards though. Critics love his music releases, but that does not always translate to winning awards.

Billboard Award

Top Rap Collaboration for "Black Beatles" | Won in 2017

Nominations

Gucci Mane has amassed a number of nominations.

BET Awards

Best Collaboration with Rae Sremmurd for "Black Beatles" | 2017
Best Collaboration with Chris Brown and Usher for "Party" | 2017

BET Hip Hop Awards

Best Collaboration with Rae Sremmurd for "Black Beatles" | 2017
Sweet 16: Best Featured Verse for "Black Beatles" | 2017
Best Mixtape for Droptopwop | 2017

MTV Video Music Awards

Song of the Summer for "*Down*" (feat. Fifth Harmony | 2017

Success Doesn't Happen Overnight

Determination, applied effort, and a willingness to change for the better describe the traits leading to Davis' success. As Gucci Mane, he has continued to develop both creative and business endeavors. He decided to return to writing, authoring his autobiography. Davis has committed to living his life in a better way. He began dieting and working out. He prioritizes his health. Determined to make it in music, he writes and produces, and he founded a record label and collaborates with others on albums. Friends in the film industry convinced him to try acting, which he had always wanted to do. It has proved a good decision, landing him job after job. Davis wanted to diversify and established a clothing company that markets affordable fashions. His is a career that took decades to build. Bad decisions made as early as junior high school contributed to the delay in his achievements. Once Davis decided to turn his life around though, he did so, even adding a strong marriage and parenthood to his life. Through each project as Gucci Mane, Davis shows the ability people have at any stage in life to change things for the better.

Davis achieved success through hard work and motivation.

Text-Dependent Questions:

1. What events led to Davis writing his autobiography?

2. What two businesses did Davis found?

3. How do Davis and his wife manage their careers and parenting?

Research Project:

Research what it takes to start a business. What would be the first step toward starting a clothing line like Delantic?

Words to Understand

Marketing strategy: The methods and mechanisms described in an organization's marketing plan to reach its target audience with its product message.

Pioneer: To develop or discover a new method or activity.

Sugarcoat: To make a fact or truth artificially attractive.

Davis is a savvy businessman, combining a dedicated work ethic, with successful marketing while remaining authentic.

Chapter 4:
Gucci Mane's Words, Lyrics, Messaging, and Brand Building

Gucci Mane's Marketing Strategy

Gucci Mane combines a strong work ethic with authenticity, diss tracks, and a professional marketing team for a successful **marketing strategy**. He has harnessed his studious nature and self-study to educate himself after leaving college early. His marketing strategy boils down to being real. He never **sugarcoat**s anything, and despite his sometimes-odd antics, his honesty brings his fans back for more music.

That Work Ethic

Radric Davis may have landed in trouble quite a bit as a younger man, but he experienced an epiphany in his thirties that truly turned his life around. The overarching thing that saved his career before that was and is his amazing, dedicated work ethic.

Davis performed at the ONE Musicfest at Centennial park, Atlanta, GA.

55

As soon as he would get released from incarceration, he would go directly to the recording studio, spending weeks and months on a creative jag. During his final incarceration, he finagled a way to get to record in jail. Over a period of a little more than two years, he released about thirty mixtapes. This constant creation meant that upon his release, he already had the rhymes ready. He merely needed to step into the studio and bust it out. In fact, less than twenty-four hours after his release from his final stay, he released his comeback track, "1st Day Out tha Feds." He emerged from a three-year federal sentence to enter the studio with some of his biggest fans—Kanye West, Drake, and Young Thug.

Scan here to listen to Gucci Mane's "Pop Music."

Authenticity

Davis's marketing team never had to create an image for the rapper known as Gucci Mane. In hip hop, especially hard-core rap, marketing teams strive to create an image that sells the person as a rapper. Since the music genre stemmed from urban streets and began as diss, typically between gang rivals, a tough image has traditionally sold more records.

As a **pioneer** of the trap genre of rap music, he illustrated the realities of street life in a neighborhood full of shotgun houses in the

Atlanta metro area. He merged the Deep South lilt of his accent with harsh realities of the drug trade, death, and poverty. His early works focused on survival of the fittest, while his later works thumb his nose at the authority figures who punished him and others for surviving however they could.

For his marketing people, the only tough part was booking tours and negotiating endorsements. They ran into amusing problems when he cleaned up. Rappers and fans claimed he had been cloned, unable to accept that they guy who had chugged lean now eats kale.

While his attitudes toward eating right and exercise have changed, his work ethic and determination have not. Days after his release, he took to the stage for an Atlanta comeback concert, billed as "Gucci Mane & Friends." Davis was joined on stage by local artist OJ Da Juiceman and rap stars Future and Drake. Stars he had yet to befriend showed up, too, like Fetty Wap. The New Jersey artist, who performs the hit "Trap Queen," calls Gucci Mane his favorite rapper. The day following the concert, Fetty Wap posted an Instagram video that showed that even the biggest stars have that hero they have always wanted to meet—the person they have always looked up to and emulated.

Davis grew up in a neighborhood of shotgun houses, such as this one.

Work Hard Dream Big

A hard childhood gave Davis the motivation to follow his dreams with determination and hard work.

Diss as a Marketing Method

Similar to the antics of Meek Mill, Davis uses diss as a marketing method. More accurately, he embraces the street method of building your own image by calling others out. In rap though, when done properly, this serves to promote both artists. Fans will often download and distribute the diss tracks created by both artists.

Davis, as Gucci Mane, has taken diss to new heights for publicity. The rapper not only beefs with other rappers, he will do so with journalists, too. So, not only has Waka Flocka Flame caught his wrath, so have podcast hosts. For instance, in an interview with Charlamagne Tha God, he continued a beef he had developed with *The Breakfast Club* hosts Angela Yee and DJ Envy in 2016. That stemmed from accusations of romantic overtures from Yee, which she denied on the air. She and Davis went back and forth for some time publicly, with DJ Envy caught in the proverbial crossfire.

Once Davis reformed his way of life, he had a representative contact Yee to provide a private apology. Yee told his rep that since Davis had humiliated her publicly, his apology needed to take place publicly as well. While in this case, the diss may have provided some coverage, it only served to create what seemed a blackballing of him from the popular show known for showcasing the biggest names in rap.

The problem was made worse by Davis's social media marketing team. Dissing on social media backfires. While they have the rapper's distinctive writing voice down, they, too, frequently engage in creating drama to boost numbers. Such was the case in the Yee/Envy/Mane fiasco. Fans were puzzled when the reformed rapper's Twitter account began posting melodrama about the years-old situation, which had begun before Davis had reformed his ways. They were accustomed to the now-adult behavior from Davis (who had married, become a full-time parent, and even reformed his eating and exercise habits), and it became the sole flub in his authenticity.

In reality, Davis was reaching out to people to apologize for the behaviors he had exhibited before cleaning up and getting sober. The rapper's social media accounts showed the one hole in authenticity and marketing, since celebrities hire someone to manage their social media. They remain busy with their professional lives and personal lives and rely on their marketing teams to manage their social media accounts, a major component of a successful marketing plan in the twenty-first century.

Scan here to watch a news report on the making of one of Gucci Mane's more unusual music videos.

Professional Marketing Team

Davis's marketing team has also worked some small wonders though, since his stage name, Gucci Mane, easily could have created a legal battle for its potential trademark violation. The marketing team, however, transformed it into a mutually beneficial endorsement opportunity with the *haute couture* design house.

It took time, but after his transformation into a clean-living family man, the rapper became a much easier sell to the design house that has been endeavoring to reach the prime Millennial market. His friendlier image helps them negotiate better deals.

This same team managed to turn a lifetime in and out of prison into a selling point from the beginning. Although it was his real life until he cleaned up, it required his marketing team's spin to keep it from tanking his career.

Fast Fact 3:

Starting a Business—According to the U.S. Small Business Administration, 50 percent of businesses fail in their first year of existence. Within their first decade of existence, most businesses–96 percent–fail. The leading cause of business failure is that no market need existed for the product or service. The second most common cause is a lack of capital leading to the business not paying its bills.

Text-Dependent Questions:

1. Discuss which Gucci Mane marketing tactic you think has been most effective.

2. How did diss as a marketing method backfire on Davis?

3. What could Davis do to solve the problems created on his social media account?

Research Project:

Choose one department in a record label, and research what it does. What positions does it typically employ? What does it contribute to the larger mission of the record label?

Words to Understand

Labelmate: A person or band who is signed to the same record label as another artist.

Outlandish: Wild, unique, or unusual.

Pugilist: One who competes as a boxer.

Stomping grounds: The area or neighborhood one regularly frequents.

Davis had a hard upbringing, consisting of poverty, hunger, drug abuse, and crime. Fortunately, he has turned his life around.

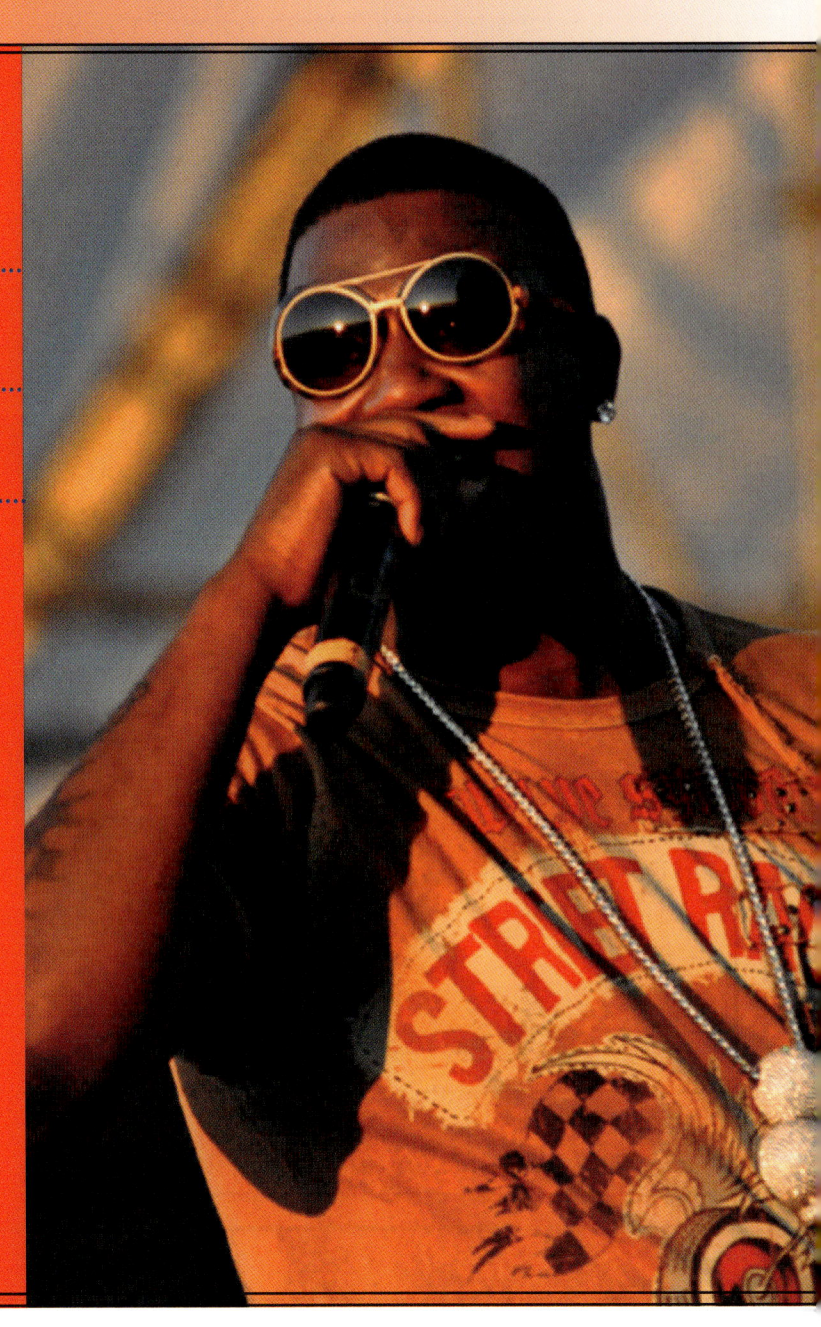

Chapter 5:
Gucci Mane Reminds Us to Give of Ourselves

As Gucci Mane, Radric Davis became known for **outlandish** behavior and raw lyric raps. Behind the scenes though, Davis supports charities and conducts philanthropy that helps children. Perhaps it is that he vividly recalls being the child who was hungry and living in a poverty-stricken neighborhood. Perhaps it is simply being a good person who wants to help others with his own wealth.

His fans must wonder, because he does not talk about it. While he promotes his albums and his businesses, he quietly goes about what he does for others. In this one activity, Davis does not brag. He simply *does*.

Actions speak louder than words. Davis's actions help children. He encourages the others around him to do the same. Many times, his donations get matched by those with whom he does business. While he remains busy in the studio, constantly working, he also makes time to support his friends' philanthropies.

The eradication of child poverty is a cause close to Davis's heart.

Toy Donations

Before their beef, Gucci Mane donated toys to the community of South Atlanta, GA, matched by a donation of Waka Flocka Flame. The donations by the 1017 Brick Squad Records owners and their **labelmates** Frenchi, Wale, and French Montana, became a topic in the documentary *Giving Back,* an M-Visions Documentaries production.

Charity Basketball

After their beef, Gucci Mane and Waka Flocka Flame put aside their differences to play together in a Charity Basketball Event in Queens, NY. That was where Gucci grew up—his **stomping grounds** before moving to Atlanta.

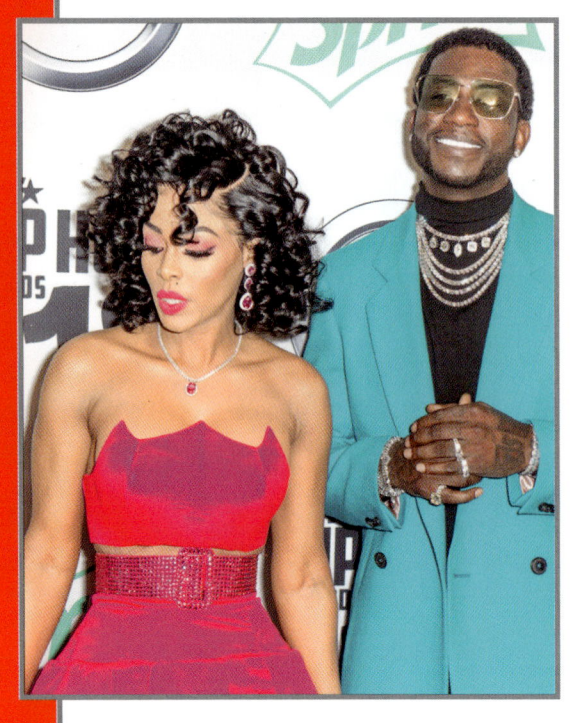

50 Cent's Second Annual 40 Day Event

The two business partners put aside their differences a second time to benefit the children of Waka Flocka Flame's hometown of Queens, NY. Gucci Mane and his 1017 Brick Squad partner donated and distributed

Family life is very important to Davis and his wife. They strive to improve the lives of kids who live in poverty.

school supplies to children in Queens as a part of 50 Cent's second annual 40 Day event. The business partners brought the then-newly signed labelmate French Montana with them to assist in providing the children with school supplies.

Boxing for Charity

Davis also offered to meet any rapper in the boxing ring for a match to fundraise for charity. He had his marketing team post the following to his Twitter:

"I'm challenging any rapper friend or foe in the ring to a boxing match. Put yo' money up. Who got hands, not raps. Who wants the challenge. The proceeds from the ring will go to charities. You scary a** Rappers."

As yet, no boxing match has occurred, but the **pugilist** is open to takers.

Fast Fact 4:

Christmas Toy Drives—Toys provide more than fun and distraction for children. They are vital learning tools that help them learn hand-eye coordination, foster creative play, help self-worth, and can provide a coping mechanism. Many families cannot afford toys for their children, so each year a number of charities hold toy drives to gather donated toys for children in their geographical area. One such organization is the Marine Toys for Tots Foundation, founded by the U.S. Marine Corps in 1947. On an annual basis, it distributes an average of eighteen million toys to seven million children. The need for programs like Toys for Tots and increased donations continues to grow.

Fast Fact 5:

School Supplies—In the U.S., fifteen million children live in extreme poverty and face challenges obtaining basic school supplies. Organizations like the Kids in Need Foundation hold annual school supplies drives to provide for these individuals. According to teacher responses to the 2018 Kids in Need Foundation School Supply Impact Survey, which queried more than 12,000 U.S. teachers in low-income communities, access to proper school supplies positively impacts their students in the following ways: improved grades, better classroom behavior, improved engagement, improved self-esteem, and better attitudes toward learning and school.

Rihanna's Diamond Ball

This is perhaps the only charity event for which Gucci Mane has been involved that would not surprise fans. He dressed up and donated to attend and offer support to his friend and co-collaborator Rihanna, who founded and organizes the annual fundraiser called The Diamond Ball. The ball funds the projects of the foundation that Rihanna began in 2012, the Clara Lionel Foundation, named for two of her grandparents, Clara and Lionel Braithwaite. Its initial projects benefitted those affected by Hurricanes Harvey and Maria. Rhianna's goal is to raise $25 million to create an emergency response fund. The Clara Lionel Foundation also created a scholarship fund and built an oncology and nuclear medicine center in Barbados, Rihanna's home country.

How Gucci Mane Reminds Us to Give Back

As Gucci Mane grew up in Birmingham and Atlanta, he not only observed but also lived the harsh realities of life in a poverty-level neighborhood in a major metropolitan city. His volunteerism and philanthropy go toward ensuring that children today do not have to experience the same hardships that he did. His efforts contribute toward children avoiding the means he felt he had to resort to in order to "keep up with the Joneses" as a child.

Scan here to watch Gucci's campaign featuring Gucci Mane.

Davis supported his friend and collaborator Rihanna with her annual fundraiser, The Diamond Ball.

Gucci Mane

Gucci Mane

HIP-HOP & R&B

Text-Dependent Questions:

1. What group of people do all of Gucci Mane's volunteerism and philanthropy benefit?

2. With which of his rap collaborators does the artist most often volunteer?

3. What methods does Davis use to fundraise?

Research Project:

Davis works to help children in U.S. metropolitan communities, such as those where he grew up and those of his business partners and friends. He volunteers and donates to charities that help solve problems he experienced as a child. What local organization could you volunteer with to help solve a problem you experienced in grade school or junior high school? How would you get started as a volunteer with that organization?

Series Glossary of Key Terms

A&R: an abbreviation that stands for Artists and Repertoire, which is a record company department responsible for the recruitment and development of talent; similar to a talent scout for sports.

ambient: a musical style that relies on electronic sounds, gentle music, and the lack of a regular beat to create a relaxed mood for the listener.

brand: a particular product or a characteristic that serves to identify a particular product; a brand name is one having a well-known and usually highly regarded or marketable word or phrase.

cameo: also called a cameo role; a minor part played by a prominent performer in a single scene of a motion picture or a television show.

choreography: the art of planning and arranging the movements, steps, and patterns of dancers.

collaboration: a product created by working with someone else; combining individual talents.

debut: a first public appearance on a stage, on television, or so on, or the beginning of a profession or career; the first appearance of something, like a new product.

deejay (DJ): a slang term for a person who spins vinyl records on a turntable; aka a disc jockey.

demo: a recording of a new song, or of one performed by an unknown singer or group, distributed to disc jockeys, recording companies, and the like, to demonstrate the merits of the song or performer.

dubbed: something that is named or given a new name or title; in movies, when the actors' voices have been replaced with those of different performers speaking another language; in music, transfer or copying of previously recorded audio material from one medium to another.

endorsement: money earned from a product recommendation, typically by a celebrity, athlete, or other public figure.

entrepreneur: a person who organizes and manages any enterprise, especially a business, usually with considerable initiative and at financial risk.

falsetto: a man singing in an unnaturally high voice, accomplished by creating a vibration at the very edge of the vocal chords.

genre: a subgroup or category within a classification, typically associated with works of art, such as music or literature.

hone, honing: sharpening or refining a set of skills necessary to achieve success or perform a specific task.

icon: a symbol that represents something, such as a team, a religious person, a location, or an idea.

innovation: the introduction of something new or different; a brand-new feature or upgrade to an existing idea, method, or item.

instrumental: serving as a crucial means, agent, or tool; of, relating to, or done with an instrument or tool.

jingle: a short verse, tune, or slogan used in advertising to make a product easily remembered.

mogul: someone considered to be very important, powerful, and in charge; a term usually associated with heads of businesses in the television, movie studio, or recording industries.

performing arts: skills that require public performance, as acting, singing, or dancing.

philanthropy: goodwill to fellow members of the human race; an active effort to promote human welfare.

public relations: the activity or job of providing information about a particular person or organization to the public so that people will regard that person or organization in a favorable way.

sampler: a digital or electronic musical instrument, related to a synthesizer, that uses samples, or sound recordings, of real instruments (trumpet, violin, piano, etc.) mixed with excerpts of recorded songs and other interesting sounds (sirens, ocean waves, construction noises, car horns, etc.) that are stored digitally and can be replayed by a triggering device, like a sequencer, electronic drums, or a MIDI keyboard.

single: a music recording having two or more tracks that is shorter than an album, EP, or LP; also, a song that is particularly popular, independent of other songs on the same album or by the same artist.

Further Reading

Mane, Gucci and Martinez-Belkin, Neil. *The Autobiography of Gucci Mane*. Simon & Schuster. September 4, 2018.

Internet Resources

www.billboard.com
The official site of Billboard Music, with articles about artists, chart information, and more.

www.thefader.com
Official website for a popular New York City–based music magazine.

www.hiphopweekly.com
A young-adult hip-hop magazine.

www.thesource.com
Website for a bi-monthly magazine that covers hip-hop and pop culture.

www.vibe.com
Music and entertainment website and a member of Billboard Music, a division of Billboard-Hollywood Reporter Media Group.

https://delantic.com
Gucci Mane's official business website for his clothing company, Delantic.

https://www.instagram.com/guccimane
Gucci Mane's official Instagram for all the latest photos.

https://mobile.twitter.com/guccimane
Gucci Mane's official Twitter for all the latest news and updates.

https://www.facebook.com/guccimane
Gucci Mane's official Facebook for all the latest news and updates.

https://www.guccimaneonline.com
Gucci Mane's official website—the go-to source for all official updates and music.

Citations

Williams, Janice. "Gucci Mane Book Review: 12 Revelations from the Rapper's New Autobiography." Newsweek. September 21, 2017.
https://www.newsweek.com/gucci-mane-autobiography-book-release-667301

"Gucci Mane Biography." All Music. Accessed Feb. 1, 2020.
https://www.allmusic.com/artist/gucci-mane-mn0000545523/biography

"Gucci Mane Biography." Married Biography. Accessed Feb. 1, 2020.
https://marriedbiography.com/gucci-mane-biography/

"RIAA and GR&F Certification Audit Requirements–RIAA Song Award." RIAA. Accessed Feb. 7, 2020.
http://www.riaa.com/wp-content/uploads/2016/02/DIGITAL-SINGLE-AWARD-RIAA-AND-GRF-CERTIFICATION-AUDIT-REQUIREMENTS.pdf

Eventful. "Gucci Mane Tour Dates and Concert Tickets." Eventful. Accessed Feb. 1, 2020.
https://concerts.eventful.com/Gucci-Mane

Lamarre, Carl. "Gucci Mane To Embark on First-Ever Tour This Spring." Billboard. February 22, 2017.
https://www.billboard.com/articles/columns/hip-hop/7694658/gucci-mane-trap-god-tour-dates

Yeung, Helena. "Gucci Mane Announces Dates for the 'Trap God' Tour. HypeBeast." Februrary 21, 2017.
https://hypebeast.com/2017/2/gucci-mane-trapgod-tour-dates

"Gucci Mane announces Canadian tour featuring Merkules & Peter Jackson." HipHopCanada. March 11, 2019.
https://www.hiphopcanada.com/gucci-mane-canadian-tour-2019/

"Gucci Mane Calendar." Songkick. Accessed February 7, 2020.
https://www.songkick.com/artists/6155469-gucci-mane/calendar

Cala, Christina and Chang, Alisa. "The Autobiography Of Gucci Mane: A Story of Rap And Rebirth." NPR. September 19, 2017.
https://www.npr.org/2017/09/19/551787647/the-autobiography-of-gucci-mane-a-story-of-rap-and-rebirth

Johnson, Noah. "Gucci Mane Is Celebrating His Freedom With a Clothing Line, a Book, a New Harmony Korine Film—and Lunch Dates with his Girlfriend." GQ. September 23, 2016.
https://www.gq.com/story/gucci-mane-style-profile

"Gucci Mane Speaks on His #SpringBreakers (Schleep) Sex Scene, and James Franco's Acting." Miss Info. Accessed February 7, 2020.
htpps://www.missinfo.tv/index.php/gucci-mane-talks-about-sleeping-through-his-spring-breakers-sex-scene/

"Gucci Mane on Spring Breakers and Sleeping Through His Sex Scene." Vulture. Accessed February 7, 2020.
https://www.vulture.com/2013/03/gucci-mane-spring-breakers-interview.html

"East Atlantic." Delantic. Accessed February 7, 2020.
https://delantic.com

"1017 Brick Squad Records. (record label)." Fandom.com. Accessed February 7, 2020.
https://hiphopdatabase.fandom.com/wiki/1017_Brick_Squad_Records_(record_label)

"Does Gucci Mane Have Kids?" Empire Boo Boo Kitty. October 17, 2017.
https://www.empireboobookitty.com/2017/10/does-gucci-mane-have-kids/

Telusma, Blue. "Gucci Mane FINALLY lands an actual Gucci Campaign." The Grio. October 2, 2019.
https://thegrio.com/2019/10/02/gucci-mane-finally-lands-an-actual-gucci-campaign/

"Is Gucci Mane Violating Trademark with His Name?" Quora. Accessed February 7, 2020.
https://www.quora.com/Is-Gucci-Mane-violating-trademark-with-his-name

Fitzgerald, Trent. "Gucci Mane Stars in New Gucci Ad Campaign." XXL. October 1, 2019.
https://www.xxlmag.com/news/2019/10/gucci-mane-gucci-collaboration/

Telusma, Blue. "Gucci Mane's rant at 'The Breakfast Club' hosts indicates how fragile he must be." The Grio. October 22, 2019.
https://thegrio.com/2019/10/22/gucci-manes-fragile-masculinity-is-on-full-display-in-new-charlamagne-tha-god-interview

Lamarre, Carl. "Gucci Mane Talks Footaction Collaboration & Why 'Atlanta Is the Mecca' for Style." Billboard. August 2, 2017. https://www.billboard.com/articles/columns/hip-hop/7881139/gucci-mane-interview-foot-action-collaboration-atlanta-style-kendrick-lamar

"Gucci Mane." Ace Show Biz. Accessed Feb. 1, 2020. https://www.aceshowbiz.com/celebrity/gucci_mane/awards.html

"Gucci Mane Talks First Grammy Nomination and Releasing His 103rd Project | Grammys 2020."Yahoo. January 27, 2020. https://www.yahoo.com/lifestyle/gucci-mane-talks-first-grammy-010158181.html

Rogo, Paula. "So … Keyshia Ka'Oir Actually Has Kids and They Were at the Wedding." Essence. October 29, 2017. https://www.essence.com/celebrity/keyshia-kaoir-kids/

Sanneh, Kelefa. "The Reinvention of Gucci Mane." The New Yorker. August 8, 2016. https://www.newyorker.com/magazine/2016/08/08/the-reinvention-of-gucci-mane

So, Daniel. "Gucci Mane Is the Latest Recording Artist to Join the Reebok Classic Family." High Snobiety. October 16, 2017. https://www.highsnobiety.com/2017/10/16/gucci-mane-reebok-lookbook/

Gucci on Twitter. Complex. Accessed February 7, 2020. https://www.complex.com/music/2013/09/gucci-on-twitter

Gucci Mane. Celebrity Endorsers. Accessed February 7, 2020. https://celebrityendorsers.com/celeb/gucci-mane/

"Waka Flocka Flame, Gucci Mane Head to Queens for Charity Basketball Event." Beats Boxing Mayhem. August 30, 2010. https://beatsboxingmayhem.com/2010/08/30/waka-flocka-flame-gucci-mane-head-to-queens-for-charity-basketball-event/

Fekadu, Mesfin. "Celebs Support Rihanna's Diamond Ball Charity Gala." Black America Web. September 17, 2018. https://blackamericaweb.com/2018/09/17/celebs-support-rihannas-diamond-ball-charity-gala/

Reid, Mitch. "Five Types of Poems." Pen and the Pad. April 17, 2017. https://penandthepad.com/five-types-poems-elementary-school-12137596.html

"Poetry sales soar as political millennials search for clarity."The Guardian. January 21, 2019. https://www.theguardian.com/books/2019/jan/21/poetry-sales-soar-as-political-millennials-search-for-clarity

World of Children. Accessed February 7, 2020. https://worldofchildren.org

"A Partial Listing of Problems Facing American Children, Youth and Families." U.S. Department of Health and Human Services. Accessed February 7, 2020. https://aspe.hhs.gov/basic-report/partial-listing-problems-facing-american-children-youth-and-families

Brunetti, Michelle. "This year, toy drives more important than ever." Press of Atlantic City. November 30, 2014. https://www.pressofatlanticcity.com/news/local/this-year-toy-drives-more-important-than-ever/article_75c9a37a-75c4-11e4-9d94-cb19530c9371.html

"History of The Toys for Tots Program." Toys for Tots. Accessed February 12, 2020. https://www.toysfortots.org/about_toys_for_tots/toys_for_tots_program/timeline.aspx

"Our Mission." Kids in Need Foundation. Accessed February 7, 2020. https://www.kinf.org/about/

"What Percentage of Businesses Fail? The Real Number." Successful Harbor. Accessed Febaury 7, 2020. https://www.successharbor.com/percentage-businesses-fail-09092015/

Otar, Chad. "What Percentage Of Small Businesses Fail—And How Can You Avoid Being One Of Them?" Forbes. October 15, 2018. https://www.forbes.com/sites/forbesfinancecouncil/2018/10/25/what-percentage-of-small-businesses-fail-and-how-can-you-avoid-being-one-of-them/#53f8b72a43b5

Lamarre, Carl. "Murda Beatz Talks Networking Skills & Collaborating With Gucci Mane, Drake & Migos," Billboard. April 11, 2017. https://www.billboard.com/articles/columns/hip-hop/7759509/murda-beatz-producer-drake-gucci-mane-migos-interview

Educational Video Links

Chapter 1:
http://x-qr.net/1J64
http://x-qr.net/1LvH
http://x-qr.net/1HzF
http://x-qr.net/1K16
http://x-qr.net/1L4f
http://x-qr.net/1K7T
http://x-qr.net/1JnS

Chapter 2:
http://x-qr.net/1KpL

Chapter 3:
http://x-qr.net/1Kfv

Chapter 4:
http://x-qr.net/1Luq
http://x-qr.net/1Kxs
http://x-qr.net/1HyX

Chapter 5:
http://x-qr.net/1JYz

Index

.45 16
1017 Brick Squad Records 47, 64
"1st Day Out tha Feds" 56
2 Chainz 12, 28
21 Savage 13
50 Cent 65

A

Addiction 46
Alabama 7
Albums
  1017 Bricksquad Presents ... Ferrari Boyz 10
  3 for Free 12
  Back to the Trap House 16
  Delusions of Grandeur 13, 24
  Drop Top Wop 12
  East Atlanta Santa 3 25
  El Gato: The Human Glacier 12, 22
  Everybody Looking 8, 10, 21
  Evil Genius 13, 22
  Hard to Kill 9, 15
  La Flare 14
  Mr. Davis 8, 12, 21
  Murder Was the Case 16
  Return of the East Atlanta Santa 12
  The Appeal: Georgia's Most Wanted 9, 18, 19, 29
  The Caged Bird Sings 10
  The Return of East Atlanta Santa 21
  The Return of Mr. Zone 6 10, 19
  The State vs. Radric Davis 9, 10, 18
  The State vs. Radric Davis II 10
  Trap House 8, 9, 14
  Trap-A-Thon 15
  Woptober 12
  Woptober II 8, 13, 24
Alsina, August 29
Anuel AA 13
Asian Doll 25
Atlantic Records 21
Awards
  BET Awards 51
  BET Hip Hop Awards 51
  Billboard Award 51
  MTV Video Music Awards 51

B

B.A. & Mook 18
Baytl 10
Beef 4 41
Bieber, Justin 13, 24
"Big Booty" 14
Big Cat Records 7
Big Daddy Kane 7
Big Tank 15, 16
Billboard 200 12, 16, 13, 19, 24
Billboard Rap Chart Top Ten 13, 14, 19
Billboard Top 20 12
"Bingo" 18
Birdman 10, 19
Birds of a Feather 41
Biz 18
"Black Beatles" 12
Black Magic 15, 16
"Black Tee" 7
Blaze-1 16
Boo 14
Brick Squad Records 47
Bryson Tiller 21
Bun B 19

C

Caesar, Jason 15
Carey, Mariah 41
Cash, Johnny 46
"CC" 13
Chill Will 19
Clara Lionel Foundation 66
"Cold Shoulder" 13
Confession of a Thug 41
Crack cocaine 7
Curve single 23

D

DaBaby 14, 25
Davis, Radric Delantic 31, 63
Davis, Vicky Dean 31
Delantic 47
Derulo, Jason 25
Diamond Ball, The 66, 67
DJ Envy 58
Drake 10, 21, 28
Dudley, Ralph Everett 31
Dutton, Jacob (aka Jake One) 22

Index

E
Essence 48
Estelle 10, 19
Evans, Sheena 37

F
Footaction 50
French Montana 65

G
Game 16
Gangsta Boo 15
Gates, Kevin 13
Georgia 7, 9
Georgia Perimeter College 36
Giving Back 64
Gladwell, Malcolm 34
"Go Head" 9
GQ magazine 46, 48
Gucci 50
Gucci Mane & Friends 57
Guwop Enterprises 10

H
Haute couture 60
Hendrix, Jimi 46

I
"Icy" 8
"I Get the Bag" 12
"I Get the Bag, featuring Migos" 9
"I Know" 13

J
Jackson, Peter 29
Jay-Z 8
Jonesboro Elementary School 32
Jonesboro Kindergarten 32

K
Ka'Oir, Keyshia 37, 44, 48
Kids in Need Foundation School Supply Impact Survey, 2018 66
Kodak Black 22

Korine, Harmony 42, 43
Kranium 25

L
La Chat 15
"Lemonade" 21
Lil Baby 14, 25
Lil Kim 16, 17
Lil Pump 24
Lil Yachty 13, 24
Lindstrom, Shane (aka Murda Beatz) 29
Luckett, LeToya 16
Ludacris 16
Luellen, Joshua (aka Southside) 22

M
M-Visions Documentaries 64
Mac Bre-Z 14, 15
Maceo 16
"Make Love" 12
"Mall" 12
Marijuana 7
Marine Toys for Tots Foundation 65
Married Biography 33
Mars, Bruno 13, 22, 24
Master P 19
Meek Mill 9, 13, 24, 58
Megan Thee Stallion 14, 25
Merkules 29
Metro Boomin 12
Migos 10, 12, 13, 22, 24, 25
Minaj, Nicki 10, 12, 19
Mixtapes 14, 26, 27
Monica 12
Moscowitz, Todd 47
"Mouth Full of Gold" 10
Musicfest 55

N
Nielsen BookScan 32

O
Offset 12
OJ Da Juiceman 19, 47
OSBS 13
Ox 18

Index

P

"Pancakes" 20
Peewee Longway 10
"Pillz (Remix)" 16
Pimp C 16
Plies 18
"Pop Music" 56

Q

Quavo 13, 25

R

Ray J 19
Reebok 50
Rich Boy 16
Rich the Kid 25
"Richer Than Errybody" 14
Rihanna 66
Rocko 10, 19
Rolodex 16
Ronald E. McNair High School 36
Ross, Rick 12, 28

S

Selassie 18
Shawnna 16
Shawty Redd 12
Shotgun house 34, 38
Slim Dunkin 20
Slim Jxmmi 22
Soulja Boy 18
Southside 13
Spring Breaker 41, 42, 43
Sremmurd, Rae 12
Supreme 50
Swizz Beatz 19

T

The Breakfast Club 58
The Weeknd 22, 23
Tours
  The Appeal Tour 29
  The Live in Canada Tour 29
  The Trap God Tour 29
Trap music 7
"Trap Queen" 57
Travis Scott 12, 21
Trey Songz 16
"Trick or Treat" 20
Ty Dolla Sign 22
Tyson, Mike 46

U

U.S. Marine Corps 65
Usher 18

V

V-Nasty 10
Verse Simmonds 10
Visual Reality 41

W

Waka Flocka Flame 10, 18, 19, 20, 47, 64, 58
"Wake Up in The Sky" 22
Wale 19
"We Ride" 12
Webbie 19
Weeknd 12
West, Kanye 8, 10
Williams, Pharrell 19
Wooh Da Kid 19, 20, 47
Wyclef 10, 11, 19

Y

Yatta Mann 15
Young Dolph 10, 12, 22, 47
Young Gunna 16
Young Jeezy 8, 9, 14, 18
Young Scooter 10, 47
Young Snead 15, 16
Young Thug 10, 21
YoungBoy Never Broke Again 14, 25

Z

Zaytoven 28

Picture Credits

Chapter 1:
Jamie Lamor Thompson | Shutterstock.com
Michael A. Walker Jr. | Shutterstock.com
Kane Udo Salters Photography | Flickr
Fabio Diena | Shutterstock.com
J Stone | Shutterstock.com
Evan Guest | Flickr
Featureflash Photo Agency | Shutterstock.com
Lev Radin | Shutterstock.com
Ovidiu Hrubaru | Shutterstock.com
Hurricanehank | Shutterstock.com
Christian Bertrand | Shutterstock.com
Jack Fordyce | Shutterstock.com
Kathy Hutchins | Shutterstock.com
Jamie Lamor Thompson | Shutterstock.com
Arturo Homes | Shutterstock.com

Chapter 2:
Arturo Homes | Shutterstock.com
Sean Pavone | Shutterstock.com
Nate Hovee | Shutterstock.com
Evan Guest | Flickr
KTDesign | Shutterstock.com
Michael A. Walker Jr. | Shutterstock.com
Michael A. Walker Jr. | Shutterstock.com

Chapter 3:
Evan Guest | Flickr
Jason Persee | Wikimedia Commons
Kathy Hutchins | Shutterstock.com
Wikimedia Commons | Fair Use
Kathy Hutchins | Shutterstock.com
Jamie Lamor Thompson | Shutterstock.com
Adam Bieladwski | Wikimedia Commons
J Stone | Shutterstock.com
Jamie Lamor Thompson | Shutterstock.com
Michael A. Walker Jr. | Shutterstock.com

Chapter 4:
Evan Guest | Flickr
Michael A. Walker Jr. | Shutterstock.com
Howard Chapman | Shutterstock.com

Chapter 5:
Jason Persee | Wikimedia Commons
Olesia Bilkei | Shutterstock.com
Jamie Lamor Thompson | Shutterstock.com
Frederic Legrange-COMEO | Shutterstock.com
Jamie Lamor Thompson | Shutterstock.com
Evan Guest | Flickr
Michael A. Walker Jr. | Shutterstock.com

Front cover:
Jamie Lamor Thompson | Shutterstock.com

Video Credits
http://x-qr.net/1J64/DJ When
http://x-qr.net/1LvH/Bangin' Beats
http://x-qr.net/1HzF/Clean Rap
http://x-qr.net/1K16/OfficialGucciMane
http://x-qr.net/1K7T /WORLDSTARHIPHOP
http://x-qr.net/1JnS/Music Is Life
http://x-qr.net/1L9u/Paul Haas
http://x-qr.net/1KpL /Chris Virgo
http://x-qr.net/1Kfv/OfficialGucciMane
http://x-qr.net/1Luq /OfficialGucciMane
http://x-qr.net/1Kxs/OfficialGucciMane
http://x-qr.net/1HyX/KPRC 2 Click2Houston
http://x-qr.net/1JYz/GUCCI

Author's Biography

Carlie Lawson began writing professionally in 1991. She spent five years at a mid-sized daily newspaper, beating deadline on a daily basis while covering politics and entertainment. She has written for monthly magazines, weekly blogs, and academic publications. Educated at the University of Oklahoma, Carlie holds Bachelor's degrees in Journalism & Mass Communication, and in Film & Video Studies as well as a Master of Regional & City Planning. Carlie owns a consulting firm and conducts research in the area of natural and environmental planning. She also owns a public relations firm. She enjoys hiking, travel, reading, music, guitar, her cat, and the positive-thinking process. Learn more at https://www.writeraccess.com/writer/13038/.